Books by J.P. White

Poetry

The Salt Hour (2001)

The Sleeper at the Party (2001)

*The Pomegranate Tree Speaks from
the Dictator's Garden* (1988)

In Pursuit of Wings (1978)

Fiction

Every Boat Turns South (2009)

all good water

POEMS BY J.P. WHITE

HOLY COW! PRESS · 2010 · DULUTH, MINNESOTA

10 9 8 7 6 5 4 3 2 1

Library of Congress Cataloging-in-Publication Data

White, J. P.
  All good water : poems / by J.P. White.
      p. cm.
  ISBN 978-0-9823545-3-7 (alk. paper)
  I. Title.
  PS3573.H4724A79 2010
  813'.54—dc22   2010023164

The author would like to thank his generous readers including Neil
Shepard, Richard Solly, Jay Hornbacher, Betty Bright and most of all Jim
Moore who helped give this book its tone, shape and final direction.

Acknowledgment is made to the following publishers from which
quotations in this collection were taken: Frank O'Hara, from *Selected
Poems*, published by Alfred A. Knopf, 2008; Anne Sexton, from *The
Complete Poems: Anne Sexton*, published by Mariner Books, 1999; and
Selections from a Sung Dynasty Poet/Su Tung P'O, translated by Burton
Watson, published by Columbia University Press, 1965.

Holy Cow! Press books are distributed to the trade by Consortium Book
Sales & Distribution, c/o Perseus Distribution, 1094 Flex Drive, Jackson,
Tennessee 38301.

For personal inquiries, write to: Holy Cow! Press, Post Office Box 3170,
Mount Royal Station, Duluth, Minnesota 55803. Please visit our website:
www.holycowpress.org

Acknowledgments

Grateful acknowledgment is made to the following publications where some of these poems first appeared:

Poetry (Chicago)
Thinking About the Enemy
White Silk (under title Beautiful Vacancy)
Southern Comfort
Lying in Bed Listening to the Ice Train
  Pass Through Wayzata, Minnesota

Southern Review
Push

Sewanee Review
The Octopus
Visiting the Wise Men In Cologne

North American Review
My Mother's Girdle

The Ontario Review
American Beach
Lights on for Safety

Great River Review
Out of the North Wind
Shy Orange Slash

Crazyhorse
Cleaning the Book Shelf
The Dancing Girls at the Diplomat

Green Mountains Review
The Origin of Farewell
The Eye of Night
Flying Over America
Stage 4
The Russian Smile

Prairie Schooner
November

Tar River Poetry
Sunday Morning in Washington Square, 1968

Flint Hills Review
The Dry-Docked Sloop

In Memory of David Wise

Table of Contents

I

God owns heaven
but He craves the earth.

—Anne Sexton, from *The Earth*

Inside Hell's Kitchen

While the worm deposits eggs in the tossed-out celery,
I draw down on a medley peddled inside Hell's Kitchen:
The *oh yeah* of a girl wearing a red bra and black shorts,
The curse knocking down a man with a push broom,
A rhyme caught in the throat of the Moroccan taxi man.
I hear something in the hip slash of the sidewalk skater
And call after her. She waves and vanishes inside a tune:
Mandarin, Switzerland, Annette, Cock, Continental.
Before heaven will suffice, I go listening for a word,
Its oily meat, its newborn orbit. Come with me, now.

Sunday Morning in Washington Square, 1968

I had just finished reading Dante's last comedy
where he says our job on earth is to gather up
God's scattered leaves, and then, with wind rising,
let them go. I was thinking about those leaves,

and the exiled poet returning home with a glimpse
of his place in the shining wheel when protestors
arrived with amplifiers, megaphones, leaflets.
A lone guitarist played a misery rhythm

way up the fret board, a blond singer in fatigues
clung to her refrain, "We gotta get out of this place."
Everywhere you looked you could see history's
unraveling sleeve, the signs of congenital agitation,

bitterness caught on the tongue like hot pepper.
That's when the NYPD rode in, swinging truncheons
and these medieval hooked lances to snag people
who had climbed the thin, yellowing poplar trees.

I was from Ohio where horses nickered behind fences.
I didn't believe police would attack unarmed people,
shovel them into gray, low-ceilinged paddy wagons.
With *Paradiso* in hand, I fled over to Bleecker Street,

where a girl I knew sold nickel spiritual pamphlets:
The Law of Pure Adjustment, Not a Sparrow Falls,
Rejoice in Your Karma, Never be Adrift Again.
I wanted to tell her what I saw. I wanted to forget.

And then I picked from my shirt a yellow poplar leaf –
its veins carried sugar, blood, brightness, shadow.
How could I carry leaves written with such oracles?
Once found and revealed, how could I let them go?

Riding the River,
Rolling the Bones

The parade up 5th Ave has no apparent end.
Drums, horns, clarinets.
Girls in fringe and feathers,
silver spangle boots,
a splash of leg and breast.

Earth Day never sounded so brassy.
One bald man in a winter coat
slips into the musical current
with a block-lettered placard,
The planet is cooked.

Walking from the East to West side,
we are like the many others –
transient earthlings, pages
torn from a book, lost notes
from up the avenue, two men

with bad ears and weak ankles
with no destination in mind.
The girl ahead of us with green hair
wears a t-shirt that reads,
Ride the River, Roll the Bones.

Her shoulder dragon tattoo spits fire.
Her green streaks sparkle.
Here we were, with her, still alive,
strolling the spring curvature
of the Park, two old friends

in the shade of a bountiful gingko,
the earth partly cooked.
I wanted to shout to all:
What a river. What a pile of bones.
What a life this is.

The Children's Barge

After a photograph by Willy Ronis

Just beyond the Île St. Louis,
a string of four, gray-slowing barges
create a curve through morning mist.
Inside the last empty barge, a boy rides
a tricycle while a second boy skips.
This hull is such a cold, hard place
with no door or window, only a skein
of laundry, a t-shirt, bra and underwear
fluttering, but not cold for these boys.
Down there inside rusted steel walls,
life swerves, dodges, leaps, races,
circles back, begins again while
the Seine holds this pair steady
and the mist blurs the next bridge
and cloaks the tender trailing aft.

Lying in Bed Listening to the Train Pass Through Wayzata, Minnesota

Some men who are at least fifty-five
wake up in the night to touch their sex
like patting the family dog on the head.
Others rise to pace the square of their den
as if called to guard duty. Still others
peer back at me from their bedroom windows
as if on lookout for some lost shipment
to arrive from Bitterroot, Montana.

I uncurl in bed listening for the 3 a.m. train
to whip through Wayzata, hugging the lake
so close I imagine it could skip the hot rails
and skid across the ancestral ice toward me,
an ice train come to ferry me home or away
from my encircling command or back to some
earlier time when I too was more fiercely
racing the night, my body clamorous thumping,
the windows rattling, the length of me
moon-drenched, snow falling, sparks raking
my wheels, one more town flown through.

At the Church of the Gladiators

It's not on any map and I probably couldn't find it again,
but it's there behind the Coliseum,
the Church of the Gladiators, the one
they came to after their battles, the one
of the black Madonna, her breasts stuck
with swords and flanked by the skeleton of a saint
trimmed in satin and gold. I sat with her
thinking there was no way out from
under the weight of history, all the layers
still intact, the basalt cornerstones and iron bars,
the battered pillars and fired bricks
buried so deep the alluvial floods
of the Tiber can't unearth them all.
And my own history, what of my arsenals,
my vast archipelago of feeble buildings,
my daggers and clubs stained with wars
I claimed I never wanted to start?
And what is beneath all my layers,
more layers, our story of the frying
of the fat and blood unending, someone
always marauding for more treasure,
and a hilltop view of the mayhem below?
And what's beneath all that withered crust:
more hiding places? And so I sat
with the black Madonna of the seven swords
and we waited, in the slow light
of a Sunday afternoon, for the gladiators
to arrive so we might touch again their wounds.

White Silk

Miami maybe where I saw her on an ocean deck.
Her legs like a lit pier running into dark swells.

I had no business inventing her history,
but how to ignore the poignant escapes

she cornered in her face, the melted interludes,
the cool struggle to turn sex into salvation.

In white silk, she weathered the hope and duplicity
I wanted to nurse inside the sun's thin shadow.

This little disappointment played out decades ago,
before I was a happy man. I wouldn't travel back there

dogged by the usual curiosities and lusts, given
to wry shifts and evasions of why I was in Florida

drifting south to islands, yet, still . . . with more lives,
I could coax the fool to say hello and tell her

it was enough, her standing there, in her plumage,
one wave tumbling while another gathered calm,

enough that she could not solve her own riddles,
my loneliness, the clever ways in which we remain

forever undelivered to ourselves, thrusted forward,
wanting to be seen, wanting to be hidden, lost

inside reluctant vacancies, proud even, and anxious
to fill the silver night with all we can't bring home.

The Dancing Girls at the Diplomat

Hollywood, Florida

Father sold a million dollars of insurance every year
and every year won a trip to the Millionaire's Club.
In 1968, the flyer boasted two swimming pools,
nightclubs, Kon-Tiki bars, dancing girls wearing
red-glazed high heels and thin black brassieres.
Eager to turn up at school in a bronze-god tan,
I fell asleep beside the pool on the first blinding day
at the Diplomat Hotel. When I awoke I was sprawled
in bed, covered in Noxzema and gauze, and a doctor
loomed saying I might bear permanent scars.
Freezing or burning up, I couldn't tell but as
my 16-year-old body floated away from me,
the news came that King had been shot on the balcony
of the Lorraine Motel in Memphis, April 4th.
For the rest of the week, hope burned down
on street corners all over America, and I lay in bed
unable to walk, and when I finally lurched forward,
afraid to touch my skin, angry with every handshake,
glance and human brush against my clothes,
father said we were going to Aunt Wilma's for G&Ts.
She had squandered the fortunes of two husbands
betting on greyhounds, puffed on black Cuban
cigarettes even though she had cancer, and father didn't
like her much. Wilma sat crooked. Too many veins
wiggled across her nose bridge and she thumped
her chest at the end of each coughed sentence.
Her two sons snickered at the celery and peanut tray,
asked me if I wanted to catch a ride in their car,
an old, long-finned, cream-colored Cadillac.
I sat between my cousins, whose names I've forgotten
or blocked out and sank back into cracked leather.
Inside, the air conditioner kicked in, screened out

the sloppy Florida air, the bunker concrete houses.
We hurtled into April twilight on a back road bordered
by strawberry patches and mosquito swampland.
Felt fine slipping into the night away from the beach,
the hypnotic pools, the heat, my parents and Wilma
whose eyes glazed over when my father mentioned King
and the smoldering riots of south Miami. As cold air
shot up my loose cotton pants, washed over my skin,
one of the cousins started drumming his fingers:
"Want to find some darkies and run them over?"
The boys howled as the big boat of a car jerked forward,
"We do this sort of thing all the time down here."
I couldn't tell if I was back at the Diplomat, dreaming
through my worst sun burnt tremors, or if I was meant
for this ride, implicated in an inexplicable crime
while I was fully awake. Summer before I'd worked
in Spanish Harlem, and spent one entire night kissing
a black girl as sweetly as I knew how, and was convinced
I could help marry the opposites of any human problem
until this man waiting beside me for tickets to the Apollo
grabbed me by the collar and said, "Listen, pretty boy,
don't ever pretend you can imagine what it's like
to be poor and black. You can't imagine shit."
But my name is White. I have white hair, white clothes,
and white skin that burns easily, so who better,
I wanted to tell him, but this impossible white boy
to sit alone, high up in the Apollo, stomping his feet
as the jumping Five Stair Steps brought their falsettos
and spin moves back for an encore. I don't know
if I actually saw a figure shadowed ahead of us
on that Florida road, but I couldn't wait for headlights
to catch his face. I grabbed the keys from the ignition,
struck my cousin in the head. The Cadillac skidded
off shoulder into barb wire. They yanked me out,
more angry with the scratched hood and busted headlight
than with the blow. "We were just kidding about niggers."
After roughing me up, they threw me aside, drove off.

I stood there for the longest time, lost on a bad stretch
of Florida road, like a sleepwalker transfixed on a balcony,
not knowing again if I was burning up or freezing,
as I looked at the cypress and scrub palms looped with nets
of Spanish moss, unable to imagine hobbling past
the charred stumps, tire treads and scattered trash,
back to the neon beaches and the Millionaire's Club
where there would be toasts, awards and much anticipation
for the plumed dancing girls who would appear later that night.

The Company We Keep

Behind each of us stands at least
one devil, one angel.
The devil says come with me
and I'll make your pain go away.
The angel says put your hands over your heart
and ask me any question you want.
No matter where we go, they follow.
None of us can travel through life
without conducting a conversation with each.
Not ready for such a private chat?
Bar the doors. Lock the windows.
Makes no difference to them.
They turn up even in the thin pocket of your bed
wanting to set the creature you are in motion.
What it will be tonight, my pet?
More questions clamped on the pulsing vein?
Or a smooth ride down without the glare of torches?

Open or Closed

Your hands are always open or closed.
They are not encumbered
with any other choices
that weight and worry the rest of you.

The bright wet fist of the infant
tells us trust comes slowly.
The outstretched fingers of the prisoner
remind us trouble finds us quickly.
How alone a person lives with memories,
dreams and pain more tangled
than the great hoop of the Sargasso Sea.

But your two hands, that old married couple,
puttering along after decades,
are still charming to watch,
one holding the screen door
while the other fishes for the key.

Mostly they are courteous, gentle and tolerant
of one another even when everything
knots your shadow and the door remains locked.

See them there by your side,
keeping you company after everyone else
has left for good, touching each other
for reassurance as if to say,
How's the weather over there?
When should we break bread?
Will this be a day to open or close?

40 Winks at the Cliff Castle Casino Hotel in Camp Verde, Arizona

The casino hotel walls, thin as a moth's wing.
A couple on the other side, in bed, their voices

cut with recriminations and a whisper of power.
Get away from me, the woman says. Some memory

of hers resurfaces with the resolve of his hand
seeking the heated depth of a fold and crease.

This constriction and failed release stalls
for long minutes, or is it hours? I get up, fling

the curtains, peer into the desert sky iced
with a million stars no one knows the names of.

I step out and hear the wind gathering bones
on the cliff, then dropping into a dry river bed.

Too many ghosts out there never going home.
Back inside, no sparks, no sweat. I grab

40 winks, wake, can't sleep, touch the wall
like a scar sealed over by neglect, wanting

to hear again their choked-off anger and regret,
how neither wanted to give in, how clearly

their *desperare* signaled they were still alive,
willing to break, hide, crawl, pay any price,

their bodies lit with the many far-dark borders
of the heart's brightness, *on, off, on* again.

The Eye of Night

When he rubbed the hospital window, he saw it:
the eye of night, immovable and enormous,
drinking in the buildings, the streets, the shops,
and the room where he lived hooked up to wires.
The eye brushed his face, absorbing through him
the face of his lover, the glare of his visitors,
the shadows of the dying in the next room who failed
to find heaven when they reached out to touch
the pale thumb of the moon. He nodded off,
looked again, and the eye was gone. What he saw
was the day flickering under the night's lash,

a day submerged in the spill of evening
and he marveled at the beauty of dissolving things,
his bowl of petals, his table of smart, unread books,
the intimate strangeness of his body secluded
from its rituals and daily pleasures. This is it,
he thought, the unzipped voyage beyond fever,
the bare-assed flight through bundled stardust,
the empty plaza at noon. But he was wrong again.
Dinner was served. The eye blinked, and he found
himself turning over inside the loneliness of night
and the long day, and the slow folding of a smile.

Hate & Envy

A letter, thrown out, returns in another box.

I don't need to read the words to picture why
you never signed it. Mexico, in the mountains
near the cold-breaking Pacific, shreds of fog.
We stopped for grit coffee and to renegotiate.
What did the man at the hand-crank gas pump say?
Turn back. This mountain road ends.
We aimed to prove him wrong with our accusations.
The more we spoke, the less we said until nothing
seemed possible but more craving and agitation.
We could taste salt air, but we couldn't see waves.

We were not alone in this first light plunder.
A pair of hummingbirds could not get their fill
of the salmon-red pomegranate blossoms.
They were drunk on pollen, yet standing still,
devouring juice said to purge the soul of hate and envy.
You took off your bra and panties. I stepped away
from my pants and shoes. We dropped to our knees,
and ate of the red blossoms scattered everywhere.

The Light Between the Mountains and the Sea

I woke in the night thinking maybe I should write an ode
to the sun caught between the mountains and the sea.
The poem would be a quiet record of the sprawling gold
in the grape fields lit with salt, mist, shell and pine.
The lines would stand inside that luster and gather
the shimmer as it expands, contracts, spills into windows,
opened doors, and into the faces of strangers eager to capture
a moment of sweetness while avoiding some memory
shining out from the vines. I know what you're thinking,
this is no way to frame a life, serving time in the space
between farewells, watching, listening, unwilling to alter
the turmoil within. And you're right, my friend,
but I was reluctant to wake or to continue sleeping
and thrilled with the writing of the poem that never happened.

On the Mexican Train

Rain in the desert, they say, is like the hand of God.

I heard that rain tapping my skull
and I woke in the dark on a Mexican train
wondering if anybody in this life
ever slips beyond the pleasures
and problems of the body.
Does anyone arrive at some other platform
where the body is not a lit fuse,
not a guttering candle,
but rather a steady light source
like the beam on the engine
of this train careening
to a one-accordion mountain town?
When the *conjunto* band starts up
and the blind pony circles the square,
can anyone find where the artesian
water climbs cold enough to make you
taste the sweet and bitter minerals?
Can anyone on this Mexican train do that?

My Lost Shoes

I loved the soft scalloped brown leather,
the sexy green tongue, the sagging arch,

the thin waxed laces, how they held me up
even when I wanted to lay my story down.

If in a hotel closet, with light bulb unresponsive
to the chain, do my lost shoes wonder

where I am, how I could have so easily forgotten
to return, seduced perhaps by a new pair?

I'm here to say I remain true to my lost shoes,
faithful to their fit. I want them to know

I don't abandon friends because they are old,
splattered or in need of immediate repair.

No matter if my shoes are on a Russian train
bound for Nizhny where we found Vera

or sitting on a Florida beach facing the Gulf
where we grit-cast my father, no matter

how far or near they may be from where
I wrestle, sleep, and pray between birth

and death on this unsponsored, blink junket,
I keep hoping against clear evidence

they will turn up in another hotel
and take me home, sure-footed,

comforted – if not forgiven for my failure
to slip them on before I closed the door.

The Bumblebee

Seems clear enough the bumblebee in June
was never intended to make
her fuzzy, barrel-chested body fly.
See her limbo the spirea,
the weight of her nearly equal
to the wonder. When I was ten,
I was electrocuted by a short
in a knotted, damaged cord,
my hands frozen to a lifeline on a boat.
I couldn't let go of the jolt.
I had to let go or die.

Then, I was flying,
not unlike the bumblebee,
my body lifted out
of the electric thrashing
into a jerky, shambling glide.
How could this happen?
The laws of electricity can't explain it.
No one saw me flying through the rain.
Did it happen? I looked down at my hands
and I remember thanking them.
And since then I now go flying all the time.

This Theory of Travel

I can't reveal the name of this island,
but it sat beneath a great round swirl of
shining blue. Where I dozed in a hammock,
a little wind stoked the pink dusty road.
I was thinking how any life begins and ends
somewhere in the middle, everything unfinished,
not fully spoken, not yet revealed on the chart,
the incompletion of our story always circling.

While I shaped and held this theory of travel,
a woman rode toward me on a bicycle.
She wore a stained blue handkerchief around
her black throat, and in her basket, three hog
snappers still bright with ocean darkness.
A sleeper on a hill, I might have been regarded
as a poor prospect to buy a fish, but no,
she had pedaled the hard hill to find me.

I wanted to wave her off, but I looked into
the flat gray eyes of her three orange fish
and I caught the tang of sweat circling
the heated stones of her breasts; she and I
now intimate and strange to one another,
buyer and seller linked by the pull of salt.
She took my hand and placed it on a fish
and I nodded yes I would take her prize.

Southern Comfort

Three turkey vultures talk shop on a sand dune.
A slow scorch inches toward the tide line.
No one knows if the hurricane will come in time
to drown the flames leaping out of the swamp.

The ancients believe the oceans remember
the shape of every hull that plies the waters.
I feel that too, sitting with you, some powers
in us may not die even after our life

slips through its wake. How else to explain
the comfort of watching you half asleep,
half drifting between this life and the deep –
your body a lens through which I see

all the boats between us, lost forever –
lost except in the ocean of memory
which is everywhere looking in the lee
for where we've gone. No one knows

what happens after the body lays down
its sorrows, not even those three vultures,
more patient than priests hunched at the altar,
each red head glistening like a peach.

The Dry-Docked Sloop

I'm *Venus* from New Orleans. Who are you?
Landlocked now seven years, my portholes
stove in, my halyards ripped down – you could
imagine here is where I'll stay, but I'll go sailing
as yesterday out over the Bahama banks, sleekly
entering coral head pools, and anchoring in
the lee of some grouper ledge until tomorrow
and a new northwesterly Trade winging me south.

My keel listens to the stories of the sea womb.
My mast touches the dark, clement skin of stars.
So turn your back, urge me to die, pity my neglect
or laugh at the enormous sealed odor I'm become.
It doesn't matter. All that's needed is dreaming
to invent a track through troubled land that will
not speak. My bow is fixed on open water.
This slowness will be lit again and made fast.

O Gulf Stream

Inside this jewel, the view is cloven, spattered, whole.
Everything electric blue in sweeping loops, rings, splits.
I swear who made thee made the spitting, doomed sun
and the blood of the dragon. Alpha, Omega, unending gyre
and witness to Pangaea – once at night, I dipped my hands
into your wet heat, cradled a bowl of luminescent plankton
that turned my fingers into ten wicks of shooting flame.
Jackknifed over the toerail, better than halfway to heaven,
I was forty miles out from West Palm Beach at night
on a broad reach for the Abacos, your acceleration
of recirculation mingling inside the oil tankers,
the pot-boiling stars, and me. I knew then I would always
return to you looking for one last call and response,
that I wanted to live and die in your saltiness born
of volcanic explosion and the galactic drag of all wind
jagged and perfect and screaming for more lives.
Used for conquest, escape, return, whale-harpooning,
turtle-grabbing, dolphin-netting, cocaine-running,
there's no holding you back or down, no force that can
outmuscle your vortices unless it might the melting
of the polar caps. Maybe ice can stop fire, maybe not.
No matter the duel, fathers and sons meet again in you.
Mine wanted to open seacocks and die in your presence
on his own sailboat, but instead we lay down his ashes
and watched him slip into your indigo on a June day
with no wind. He would have preferred rough seas,
a night not fit for a beast, and not the heated, blue coil
of your welcoming, drawn bath. On another summer day,
I too will join him, and travel due north on fire, please, again.

II

Have you forgotten what we were like then
when we were still first rate
and the day came fat with an apple in its mouth . . .

—Frank O'Hara, from *Animals*

My August Susans

Planted in late August heat then left for a week,
my overlooked Susans packed on a wagon,
one at full price, the second for a penny,
seemed beyond repair when I returned from Oregon,
their leaves shrivel-burnt, their lower buds tight
as asphalt stones, their stems drooped toward dirt,

all spark driven from their limbs. Then a front
of straight line winds, a slashing rain, a seasonal shift
all in one night, and my belief, lying in bed lit up
with lightning, I would find them buried in mud,
in need of rooting out. Out to grab my paper,
I see all twelve of them standing up under rain,

their curled leaves still brown, but now with a perky,
come-hither legginess, a new wink in their eyes,
a single ripple of muscle in their stalks, all of my Susans
flickering, curving loose-jointed with a willingness
to enter September wearing that perfect yellow dress,
backless, sleeveless, held up only by invisible strings.

Push

I'm down in the lane, counting laps, dividing the blue line
on the pool's floor with my breaststroke, aiming to loosen
my shoulders, tight as sun-stretched leather. Two women,
maybe sisters, one blind and holding onto the other's arm,
trudged into my lane to exit on the ladder. Because of earplugs,
I can't hear what they're saying, but I can tell this maneuver
is an enormous mountain. As I near them, the thin woman
motions for me to help her lift the other woman up the ladder.
As though a common request, she frowns when I don't seize
the left buttock and lean my head and shoulders into the flesh
of the woman stuck on the ladder. "Push," she whispers.
"Harder. You can do it," and so I take up a weak challenge,
hurting as I do with my own pain, and both of us brace
beneath the burden of this woman's behind. We grunt,
splash, nudge her up a rung and out. Coughing, sputtering,
I half-expected a nod of complicity, but the thin woman
shot up the ladder as though our bodies had shared too much
and only embarrassment could be left. The blind sister
on the ladder must have topped 300 lbs., a weight demanding
faith to navigate the demand of seconds, each one a solitude
impossible to grasp. Her paper-white knees rubbed as she walked,
a wobble threatening tilt. Her hands swollen, blotched, tiny.
As she inched toward the showers, I saw how hard it is
to release the mind's tonnage, its daily dose of recriminations,
judgments, its delirious grip on the body as vehicle for grace
and approval. Pain connects, we're told, but for how long,
when the riddle of our story encircles like a moat? For that look,
everything was alien to me, her trial, my own, and the unanswered
gravity of it, but then, after she was gone, I saw her again
in my hands, the great balled density of her rising up, rolling back,
rising against the odds to merge with the day she found,
such as it was, perilous and unplanned, radiating clemency
and comedy, unspoken, no eye contact made. *Push. Harder.*

My Mother's Girdle

At ten I felt privileged to wander
my mother's room and watch her getting ready
to go out, snatching clothing from hooks, leaning
into her mirror to layer on the first coat of makeup,
dressed only in a beige girdle that made
an already slim woman look slimmer still.

I didn't connect her long-line bra with sexiness
nor did I regard the rigid stretch of her undergarment
as an essential compliment to her figure.
Grateful only I could spend time in her room,
chatting about the day, mine and hers,
the garden club or rummage sale fundraiser

she was half-rushing to get to, the fate
of my baseball team that needed much more
than good pitching, both of us relaxed yet in motion,
her body in a twirl, mine lounged on her bed
as I watched her slowly become the woman
who could slip a room on the tongue of a breeze.

Today's news says the girdle is coming back
to hide the unbecoming bulges of the boomers.
If my 85-year-old mother were so inclined
she could choose from leg slimmers that resemble
footless pantyhose, body-hugging camisoles
that smooth extra flab on the back and stomach.

She could contour her body with more comfort,
but all this fuss and bother is just about gone
and now she seems lighter on her feet
than a bantamweight in the first round.
I stand naked before the mirror every morning
and makes wishes for my body

that should embarrass a grown man given
to memories no one else can share.
What more can I tell you? I miss
watching my mother trim her body
while she took time to reveal stories
about unhappy friends and neighbors

she might otherwise not have told,
her voice, intimate and free and soothing
as it mapped the silhouette of trouble
and joy and all that lies between.
Nothing was hidden those mornings
as my mother angled the mirror to her liking.

Which is maybe the great blessing of underwear.
Before the world judges your shape and size,
before the room welcomes or shuns you,
before the need for style pinches at the waist,
you can speak plainly to a loved one
about the coming journey of a single day.

Human Form

It's not easy to live in human form.
All those meals. All those days
looking for work or working late
because we have no one to play with.
All those blue crumbling laundry pellets
and those changes of underwear.
All those invisible chains from childhood
and late promises too soon broken.
All those opportunities for revenge
boiling the skull. All those hours
we must sleep only to face again
the tired stranger in the mirror
who argues one home
is not just as good as another.

It's no wonder some choose to leave
the planet early and dissolve
into the sky like my friend Ray
who said death wouldn't be so bad
if you desired it, so he hit everything
hard until all the edges cutting him
softened, and his prayers bent back
their own echo saying God lived
at no fixed address, so he climbed
out onto the ledge, near dawn,
and released his hands from the railing
like a man who decides
there's no point in fighting
with a snarled garden hose.

American Beach

This morning's nor' east surf kicks up shells.
Vultures in the saw grass hobnob
round a spent pelican,
their heads like flares lit in the blue-black sky.

Death rides on the bright road of foam
and feeds more bald, high-flying life.
I count six eaters aproned
in feathers and blood.

Next dune over,
American Beach, the last black-owned town
on the Atlantic seaboard, leans
closer to growling combers

and weighs the sands of the changing bight.
Carolina's Seabrook and Kiawah
caved in to whites
who gained ground with golf, condos, taxes.

American Beach is next.
I can see the downward spiral in squat cinder block,
swinging doors and ghosts
who can't outlast tomorrow's 18th hole.

Wedged between Plantation resort to the south,
where my parents own, and the Ritz looming
like an Alps villa in the north,
American Beach once packed

its beachhead and juke joints
with Louis Armstrong and jazzed blacks from Tupelo,
who felt safe enough to dance fast
through slow, segregated decades.

After the marches, a black exodus shimmered
to the tough Northern cities
because the wide world's rim
could not be pinned to a beachfront dream.

Now, Nassau County won't pave the streets,
pay for sewer treatment or 911.
Fenced out by opulence, these sand hill cottages
flap like old bellows above embers.

Glossy ads show *Amelia the Grand*
with world class golf, tennis courts,
health clubs, miles of trucked white sand
packed hard like marble floor.

It's all of that and more which I favor
as do middle-class blacks from Atlanta
and Birmingham. But like the air
cut with acrid paper mill undercoat,

this glittering sand rolls back to when ships
deposited dead slaves who didn't fair the crossing.
It's the one inescapable script
coiled inside the empty bottle at my feet:

Beauty will always erase the scribbles of history
and sell it as vacation land,
a whitecap Heaven dredged from misery.
New condos sparkle at Plantation Point.

Magnolias flavor salted air
and crowd a black cemetery tucked under maritime oaks.
At the white beach, lounge chairs,
umbrellas and cool drinks rake into place.

Children squirm under layerings of oil.
Threads of mist climb and tangle
over fast running swells
that suck the sand from beneath my feet.

More vultures arrive from the distant smoky interior
to feed on the fallen pelican.
They fold together in a greenish pool of shadow
as if in a cathedral of very high windows.

Flying Over America

January's claw can't scrape the snow-dusting
on the hard crust of the long body of the land.
All of Ohio, Indiana, Illinois, Nebraska, Iowa,

cast through the tripod of civil engineers
and surveyors, the land cut into squares,
thin strips boxed by rural routes, barb wire,

parceled and recorded at county courthouses
to be bought, sold, disputed by previous owners,
each farm and homestead locked as a Abstract

of Title inside vaults, the land itself stamped on
scrolled certificates, staked by law, stoplights
and four-way stops, but in time it won't repeat

like this from the sliver window of a jet, in time,
whatever is held in deed, trust or title, whatever
the plat reveals about the correct representation

of boundaries and all visible encroachments,
all of the feet and inches will not hold in place,
and the land, at some future date, will outshine

the scored lines and return to its original flow
and unbounded strength, nothing named, divided,
and given over to enclosures, edges, borders,

the place once more rounded by wind rustling
back from the last reaches of the world, the darkness
breathing again with the yelping of animals.

The Russian Smile

You see it mostly in June when the brides
are everywhere in white soaking up
as much sunlight as cloth can hold,

the grooms off to one side, smoking,
reluctant to be exposed to the lens
when the camera has never been kind.

In every town and every city you find
memorials to war dead, so many millions
there are not enough ledgers to contain

them all, not enough human memory to hold
all the fathers, uncles, wives, children.
Even now most of the beds are too short

because the carpenters built all the frames
to lay down men stunted by stone soup.
Within the thick walls of birch and pine,

the past is never a door easily entered.
The future, always a kicked explosion.
So the smile lives so far back in the soul

only a rarity will bring it forward
like when the bride lifts her gown to reveal
a pink garter, the tease of what's to follow

seen in the flare of her hand, the groom
biting down on his teeth, then grinning, or here
on the street, the pinched and stooped elders

watching a girl in a summer dress playing
a fairytale mouse, the one with the least power
who releases the grip of the giant turnip.

Lincoln's Hat

There are breathless curios to find in D.C.,
documents, memorials, portraits, the two
magnolias planted by Andrew Jackson.
Surprisingly, the best of these are free.
Of them all, I wanted most to spend time
looking at his eight-dollar stovepipe hat,
where he kept jokes, crib notes for cases,
musical phrases he aimed to combine
into speech, and that he wore to the farce.
Clearly, he favored its height, needed
to feel bound to the ribbon brim-wrapped
in Willie's memory. Age brings a sparse
welcome to black silk; now it bleeds
the color of a penny out of circulation.
He talked of wanting to see California.
His prized, plug hat never left the theater.

The Hospital of the Innocents

In every city, in every country,
in every season, in every age,
they are left on bridges, on crossroads,
in the deserted places and well-traveled ones.

They are left on grilled window ledges,
in reed boats, inside marble basins,
at the steps of convents. They are left
at train stations and apricot orchards.

They are left anywhere people gather
and disperse, under bridges, inside gardens.
They are left at the meeting places
between three living men and three dead,

left at the stables, at the grape harvest,
at the mouth of the sea of the Leviathan.
They are left under the portico
of the thin, nodding Elders, the numbers

of abandoned infants countless, unending,
mostly newborn, others just months old,
all naked and kicking, a vast spiral
of round, unblinking faces, so no matter

where you turn, peering up or the long way
down, you see them caught between
the dark shining wheel of infernal slaves
and the army of angelic cohorts,

everything in their compact bodies
perfectly assembled and unfinished
and needing sustenance, each a messenger
from another lost story, each one broken

and aching to emerge from stone,
each a triumph over the coming end
of the world. So who will stop and open
the satchel, the box, the bag?

Who will allow new life to come forth
out of the scream? It could be you
or together we could untie the bundle,
unpack the riddle, undo the knot.

No matter the hour, the child must be
reborn because without her, your soul
and mine is incomplete. Without her,
the next door cannot be opened.

The light cannot make its square upon
the inner walls. Without her, the day
will not release its weight and begin
again. Without her, there at your feet,

dirty, squirming, fisted and shaking
with the tintinnabulum of a long distance
hunger, nothing clear and present
is possible, and the bells will not ring.

Adam's Extermination

Some October mornings there are more crows
than fish in the sea. Everywhere they circle,
swoop and corner anything that doesn't look
like them. Lying in bed, I say to the universe
let them have whatever they came for.
The earth needs more disposal artists.

The red squirrel who sleeps belly up
on the high fork of my walnut tree
doesn't care much about death or taxes
or who the next President will be.
He is nut-stuffed, nearly sick, but happy
to strip the fruit and feed himself more.

Driving home in the drizzle surge gray,
I'm passed by Adam's Extermination van,
whose tag line reads, *There were pests
even in the Garden of Eden,* and I think
kill them all Adam, kill the spiders,
centipedes, lady bugs, mice and roaches

eager to find a new winter home, kill
because we all must do it well. We kill, eat
and toss the bones and call it a day's work.
The crow says, yes. The red squirrel nods.
I once loved the idea of Eden, free of
stairwells, porticoes, arches, colonnades

of marble statues, but I hadn't considered
pests, and Adam's need to exterminate them.
I hadn't thought propellant gas was necessary
back then, only whimsy and wonder like:
Give me more of this, less of that.
Give me the girl in the strawberry hat.

Visiting the Wise Men in Cologne

We arrived late at a small immaculate hotel.
Like most we'd come for the cathedral and tomb
Of the three wise men. The young owner
Wore a puffy silk shirt, and in all rooms
Swayed handsome inside plumes of smoke.

The next day, before we set out, we saw photos
In the breakfast nook of a tennis player – headlines,
Trophies, fawning women, sleek cars – evidence
Of fame, the accoutrements of a lavish style.
The star was the young man's grandfather –

The thick black hair, high forehead and
Easy smile, identical. Riding on family
Fame, the young owner had already mastered
The jubilation of the blurred sweet life
Without ever having gripped a racket.

We could picture him routinely eating late,
Smoking and drinking after the cafes closed,
Driving a peppy sports car, keeping women
Charmed with his insouciance, his disregard
For boundaries, appetites, signs of distress.

We talked about the drug of extravagance,
The thrill of speed as we aimed for the cathedral,
Stained nearly black by pollution and nailed
Above the Rhine like a lacy bat's wing.
Did I envy the purity of his abandon

As much as you rejected the kissed promise
Of the greater life rushing toward this man
Through women he would never love enough?
Did I crave the pleasures of my younger self
With no intention of telling you I felt lost?

Inside, the basilica flamed radiant as hydrogen,
Encased in gold, silver, and jeweled enamel.
Brighter still were the faces of pilgrims
Who saw in the tomb a shining child
Waiting for the beginning of the world.

Lights On For Safety

Florida road sign

High-balling semis packed with oranges
Nearly blew me off two-lane blacktop.
No room for error. No shoulder.
Tire tread everywhere dropped

Off hubs like belts of ammunition.
War lottery numbers rattled
My head. How high would they snake
Into my future, did luck even matter?

From home in Lauderdale to school
In Sarasota, I clutched the wheel,
Drifted between historical afflictions
And the prehistoric meal.

There, see them, walking catfish
En route to Lake Okeechobee,
The armadillo scuttling, its oily
Perfume slicked against smoky

Swampland somewhere burning.
I flipped headlights on by noon.
August heat rippled asphalt
Thick with gasoline fumes.

Turkey vultures hung in currents
Spiraling above road kill,
Piloting forever in one circle
With the precision of gun milling.

The floor of the world sweated fire.
Hot-boiled peanuts, airboat rides,
Confederate flags – road signs pulled me
Beneath a bird's supple climb

High into a haze-thermal pocket.
Boys with different numbers would die
Strapped to the curl of a flame.
Who, what, where – the old cry

Flies up from every creature,
Even from a vulture accidentally clipped
Feasting the road, its throat dipped red,
Its eyes against the windshield stripped

Into mine across the greatest possible distance.

Shy Orange Slash

Oh go ahead, dump it, dredge it, spew it, spray it,
choke it, sink the piling as deep as you can.
Build a better spaceship the size of L.A.
Send a wedding invitation to Mars.

Exactly 3.7 miles from this wetland fox run,
I-494 lies splayed for an extreme makeover.
Beneath a spanking power grid, hundreds
of heavy equipment operators tear a gash

so the highway can funnel more cars to the burbs.
There's some beauty in this excision as the scrapers,
excavators, crushers, graders, compactors, backhoes,
boom cranes and dump trucks grind out linkage

between bridges and exits. All this work under
welded sparks will serve for a while to feed
us in and out of the balling metropolis, and praise be,
I will hug the curving speed of the new silver

conduit as much as anyone. This is Minneapolis,
but it could be Denver, St. Louis, Las Vegas.
Everywhere the race is on to cut corridors
so more of what we are loops toward the fox,

who worries today about the crows hectoring her
across James to Highland Avenue. Maybe
she's smoking some enemy away from her den
or maybe she craves an early morning harbor view

where the narrow sloops tug at their moorings.
Where she goes, we can't follow and yet we do,
we will, we are already behind her, and in front,
the shy orange slash of her painted on the woods

even after her ringed tail flips past the corner lilacs.

November

It takes a bang in the head from a cocked door the cat pushed open
to love what the Chinese call the season of damp-cold invasion,
this ghostly framework of slick trees providing shelter for no toad,
nothing to cut the gray until the snow burns light against all that falls.
But wait a minute, what of those chatty physicians, the Canadian geese,
zipping at treetop, crisscrossing rubble, kneading the knotted body
of the world below with their wingtips, each honk a recognition that still
something lives, even at the cost of a deep-bone shiver that won't let go?
Wake up, hold on, gulp air they say from their vibrating filament
of muscle and bone. Everything will soon be submerged, oozing
and unreachable in the human soul, everything will be ending, but not yet.
There's time to float with us into the lost shining beneath the shade,
time to raise up inside the wall of drizzle and gaze into spitting sky,
time to hear: *Dark as day is, your pulse is still a jailbreak in the throat.*

Thinking About the Enemy

In the beginning we could hear their swords cutting jewels
From the protected orchard while our children heard fine teeth
Dragging along empty granary floors. Between us and them
Stands the great wound, swallowing all tears, all voices.

Transfixed or transformed by this pain? We never know because
Who can slip through the gate without throwing a shadow
Toward both the past and present? Fire, flood, famine –
All we've wished upon them a thousand times, still they inch

Back and taunt us with their persistence. We track them down
To a quick end. More come. And the old memories grow new.
The future seems already written with a pen of iron. The book
Unreadable, immense. The enemy has become our masterpiece.

Last Entry in the Logbook

Here the outer bays are mirror-smooth
And we'd been right to say out of the north wind
Comes splendor because the enemy fleet
Was now dispersed and the possibility
Of some other landing spliced itself
Into the white-sprayed coastline.
So much violence preceded that moment,
Still held taut in our spines
By the enduring threat of its outbreak.
But now we caught the smell
Of vanilla bean and hibiscus
And watched purple-throated hummingbirds
Swerve through the luff of our topsails.
We looked toward land, believing
If ever a change could happen, now
Was the time. Now we might
Retrieve our former messages
From the steel-blue loneliness of the sea,
And no longer kill the things we love.

III

The clear wind – what is it?
Something to be loved, not to be named . . .

—Su Tung P'O

Every Secret Thing

In those days and in that farewell time,
I could hear a voice telling me to get up.
Hurt and scared is not enough it said.
But then when I stood,
I took three arrows to the heart:
This is how the world is.
The sea is not yet full of your sorrow.
The crooked will not be made straight.
Which is when I set out in a small boat
because who can make sense of the wolfish land?
I wanted the break to shove me into a new wind,
turn me into a new, unregistered blue
born of salt, wind, the pure thrill of the storm.
Hunger then, hunger now
to outlive the apocrypha
and enter the stronghold of every secret thing
waiting just beyhond the doom
to greet you and me, and all the unseen friends we have.

The Smile That Opens the World

I had nearly forgotten the familiar slouch, how his beard
drew light to his eyes. I needed his flushed and reckless laughter,
to sit near him, so I would gain strength to face the days ahead.
But he spoke of a bad turn in the hospital and said it had been years
since he smiled upon his aimless walks through Hell's Kitchen.
We sat at the cafe, the rise and fall of our chests almost imperceptible

as if we were prematurely dead and didn't know how to describe
such a vigil fused with the pledge to be grateful we were still alive.
And yet, just that little shared breath was an up-flickering that fueled us.
Leaving our table, I saw the slow curve of his lips and I smiled back
at my friend and held that smile open for all the men and women
worried on the sidewalk, strangers no longer, and all the way home.

Cleaning the Book Shelf

On the back cover of *Henderson the Rain King*, I'd scribbled
"Pick up your ticket in the urinal, set sail for Morocco,
visit Rimbaud's fabulous pig opera." No wonder my father

wanted me to switch majors if I was writing such slippery
arcane footnotes and telling him I needed more money
for books. But I took my scratching seriously, told

friends I would curl my lion's tail around the night's
disharmonies and wake up with a pair of wings. Mostly,
I propped up a bartender's elbow in Sarasota, stood watch

on the hours between midnight and dawn, waiting to take home
some lost image to help me confront the slumbering seed
of things, or at least that was my line when I grew tired

of hearing this battered green parrot scream, *Whack his pee-pee*.
Every so often, I would like to go back to a waterfront bar,
try to fix a situation, make an offering of some meager kind

to the places and people that dissolved into watery portraits.
This happened the other day, when cleaning my bookshelves,
I found a photograph of a Spanish woman I'd met in the islands.

I'd left in a forty-foot trimaran from Georgetown, crossed
the Thorny Path to Hispaniola en route to the Virgins in March.
The trade winds, so constantly pulling from the north, switched

during crossing, and the skipper and I took wind in the teeth.
Our boat blew a hatch on the starboard pontoon, and she started
listing badly. We radioed into Cuba and the Dominican Republic

but no one, not even the military patrol, would risk coming out
in such high seas. We hobbled toward Puerto Plata. By dawn
we knew it lay too far off, so we found on the charts

the port of Luperon, where we had to sail between reefs
to spot the harbor entrance. Once in the channel's lee,
dark blue water glassed over. We saw men and women paddling

canoes to greet us. We were offered bottles of local rum,
a pure blackstrap that hit the throat like a struck match.
We were given horses and fed lobsters roasted on the beach,

and when the mayor learned I had brought a guitar,
the townspeople gathered in the square to hear me strum
my three good chords. The women tried to teach merengue.

You couldn't take a shower anywhere or find a laundry
but every night, bars were jammed with milky-brown women
in brightly-lit dresses dancing this limping, two-step shuffle

that made my voice zigzag and bump against my windpipe.
I couldn't get the moves right – simple, smooth like a bolt
of cloth that just kept rolling away across the floor.

Inside the cheese-grater rasp and drag of that historical music,
I met this women with black-cropped hair, her skin the color
of cinnamon and cocaine. She could have crawled that night

out of an oil drum, or just stepped off the deck of a cruise ship.
I couldn't place her age. She motioned for me to dance,
pressed her hips against me, rocking, rotating, nearly percussive.

Later, we ate grouper with ginger and coconut, topped
with a scoop of mango sherbet. After we finished a bottle,
she said she needed money, so I gave her a ten dollar bill.

When I slept in her tin shack perched on cinder blocks,
I should have found a way to offer more than cash.
I should have written a song, listened to her complaints,

dreams, composed a letter in my scattered Spanish
slipped it into one of my empty rum bottles and thrown it
into the sea. I might have helped her stitch mosquito netting

which kept falling around us, or repair the rusted, sagging
corrugated tin roof. She asked for little. I gave less.
My head spun from the dance steps as I listened to the rattling

of the calabash gourds that hung in bunches from her porch.

The Octopus

Maybe the short life of the octopus
is best as she clings to the cave wall.
In three years she gets three hearts
and spends them all. Her final act
before dying is to blow hatchlings

from her door. You might think
she recoils into too much darkness,
yet with very little slippage, unlike
my father, eighty-nine now, repeating
bits of story into one *non sequitur*.

It hurts to watch him stagger into dotage,
when he claimed, like so many others,
he would never let this crimped, jabbering
man find him. A sailor all his life
in love with the buried lee rail, now

he withers at the slightest Florida snap.
I walk the beach to escape the cave
of his fuzzy brain, angry with myself
for my impatience with his patter.
I don't pan for the black shark's teeth

he asks about as if they were pearls
to buy him one more trick at the wheel.
Instead, I picture the octopus,
living out past the string of shrimpers
dragging their rusted iron doors,

her suction-cup arms holding fast
to the inky deep-sea ledges
but not for long or just long enough,
her last heart giving out as her young
spring free for the scramble, suck, pull

of this brief, beautiful corruption.

To Catch a Boat

The end always near no matter where you start.
Driving east out of Vermont on Rt. 89
to catch a sailboat in Nantucket, bound
for Bermuda, an October delivery for cash,
I saw a rip of chrome burning a hole
on the highway and swerved
just as a wrong-way drunk clocked by,
and slammed into a trailing car,
a woman, the State Patrol told me,

about my age, the wreckage so loud
and immediate I thought a meteor had
smacked into the granite ridge Vermont is.
After telling my story to the authorities,
I drove on, seeing in the rearview,
how the end and the beginning
are not broken by the long in between,
but are forever wrapped around the other
like twins of the same hard shine.

My boat in Nantucket never entered the gash
of the open sea. A front swept in,
stalled over the oldest whaling island.
The swell's comb chafed every snugged line.
The captain wanted to sit out the weather
by drinking dark rum below decks.
I had told a woman I loved and feared
I was going back to sea where I belonged.
Having once tasted flight, I wanted only

the 600-mile run out past the Gulf Stream,
the water so blue in its roiling tonnage
it stings just to look at the maw of it.
I jumped ship, turned back for Vermont,
impatient with the captain, he with me,
my hands again trembling the wheel.
I had to start over for blue water
by slipping back into mountains.
The sea's solution would have to wait.

The gold leaves took a knock down from the rain.
The wind whipped a terrible engine noise.
Sea brink and summit held me to the road.
I looked again for a Lucifer match flickering.
All sailors know there's another reef ahead.
The land is more dangerous than we know.
There would be no more telling
the beginning from the end.
I would never tell anyone about this voyage.

The Origin of Farewell

The boy mills the docks, eyeing the sails
Folded over booms, believing water beyond
Is better than the grasp of stinking fish stalls.
He's heard of islands like leather-lung billows
Throwing sparks off cliffs, icebergs with eagles,
Valleys cut with waterfalls and ginger lilies
That restore sight. He sees in sailors' faces
That the flight into the serpentine line of winds
Is not enough. Beauty is not enough.
Their hands are raw from splintered wheel.
Their faces burnt from unbridled visitations
At the periphery of what they dreamed
Could save them from sailing home mortal.

Still the boy leans toward the graveyard watch,
This reaching after remoteness, voluptuous
And unchanged. What else can he do
But wait his turn to be swept into the flood?
This going out is the only law ever whispered
Over tables by the ones shot with memory
Of blue-black storms. Soon, he'll know
The hymn that opens and closes the circle
Of a voyage. Until his shipping out, he'll watch
The harbor swell with jugglers, stevedores,
Women with bright keyhole lips who make
Of farewell, a vigil – *Not yet, come back.*
Everything you want is already here, right here.

On Any Given Day

Out for a morning walk, the wind just laying down
a crease on the lake, I greet a neighbor shoveling mud
after the first downpour in months. Between scoops,
he tells about Tim who drowned in Carson's Bay
on Saturday night after waking on his sailboat to take a leak,
tripping, conking his head, plunging overboard.
No one on the boat, nor on shore, heard the thunk and splash.

An older father, like me, Tim met his son everyday at the bus.
He took the boy swimming, boating, fishing
and he played ball with him in the park.
He was always the Dad – tough, tender,
nothing held back by glancing at his watch.
At the beach I've watched Tim rub his boy's head
with a towel until his son yelped for him to stop.

I knew nothing about Tim's habits, his moods, nothing
about his inner life nor how he kept vigil with his life's knots.
All I know is the seven-year-old son will not have his father
waiting at the bus, and all the boy's thinking about everything
will be forever altered by his father's one misstep.
When I walk past Tim's house, I look for the boy behind the screen.
My steps say: look, don't look, look, don't look.

Same day, at the State Fair, I watch a first time mother pig called a *gilt*,
slabbed in a pen, strain to give birth to the fifth in her litter.
Where any animal might seek the quiet of a barn,
some privacy, the light dim and forgiving,
this gilt is hemmed by hundreds of viewers,
many of them children who eyeball her in a mirror
or on an overhead TV screen, the camera lens shifting

between the live, staggering and sucking piglets
and the isolating throb of her cervical muscles.

When she grunts and pushes, I see a faint ripple jump
at the upper end of the uterine horn, and I picture her fifth
squeezing through blood to the other end of the canal,
wondering if her piglet tangles in legs or wraps itself in cord,
the crowd and I knotted and looped, fixed and fluid.

The first birth cycle, I'm told by a microphoned woman, is the hardest,
but after that, the litters are larger and easier to drop,
the birth canal now stretched, toughened for the litters ahead,
the gilt now a sow, seasoned in the common trials,
her memory a source of strength for the expectant quivering,
and I think no, it's always hard to come into this world,
hard for the mother and child, hard for the father,

everything we do is much harder than we can imagine
no matter our momentary blindness or full awakening,
just as it must be hard to leave, even when it's quick and unforeseen,
even when no one is witness to the aperture, even when
the wind rattles the halyards and tells you the lake is ready
for your sails to fill, and for the next day to come on
even when a voice says, *look, don't look, look, don't look.*

Happiness is a Boat to Anywhere

Before my shipwright father left the earth,
he went back to a crosswind nibbling his ear,
telling him to kick off covers
when he was eight, throw open the screen
and run to shore where a Canadian gale
had sputtered out before dawn. There,
an oak door spit out by the chop.

Salvage belongs to gulls and early risers,
now his for dragging over dunes,
planing into keel timber, sister ribs,
planking, a first sailboat. But how
did he know to shape a door into a hull
for bed sheet sails? He never learned
such a trick from a bookish father.

How did he know he could send out
any pain through his hammer and chisel
and have it gathered up in the immensity
of water? Then, as now, he put his hands
to work in the wood of dreams, stepped
through the oak door into the tired jag
of Lake Erie, blinked once, and was gone.

Conversation for Another Day

He did not have to breathe.
The night breathed through him
Until he was no longer afraid
Of its immense closeness.

He did not have to say more
Or open his eyes. He did not
Have to make good on his promises.
He was fast moving invisibly beyond

This brazen and commanding world
And he seemed surprised that the end
Was being arranged for him.
The darkness of his body brought

Its own balanced order, each
Of us bent down and listening
To the flickering of his eyelashes,
Thinking this moment of departure,

Streaming in and out of shadow,
Was also something else, a place
Of safekeeping, a source of,
How else to say it, well-being,

That his final nod was not a helpless
Flutter, but that part of the story
Where the flow of night brings comfort
Because there's no end to its reach.

My Crocodile

This has been a rare bright season in the underworld.
Several shadows have unlocked. More monuments have fallen.
My dream journal tells me over steaming oatmeal to keep
the pure discontent of not knowing intact. Anything can happen.
Vengeance. The unsalted truth. More secrets. Burnt toast.
I had a dear friend who went over to doom and he wanted me
to go with him into the old river mud. Oh, he was convincing
in his description of how we've wrecked the earth, how there
was nothing to be done but watch the cosmos reform itself.
Now, it's more than possible, cataclysm is coming but the end
has always been tomorrow or yesterday, so I challenged him
to come over for buckwheat, cinnamon pancakes, and help
the sunken, one-eyed world to imagine love without sorrow.
But I asked too much of him, and now he's gone and I'm the one
who has lost my sad, drifting crocodile who thought nothing
of leaping at comets. If you see him, ask him to come home.

The Day You Can't Replace

The dying will tell you when it's late or soon.
Some will take more water, some less food.
Some will stare at the walls like windows.
Others will get lost in their own room.

The dying will show you how much goes wrong.
They will sleep during the day, wake at night.
They will cry when others are given to laugh.
No one can explain how they've lived this long.

The dying will take you to the precipice.
They will unlock sparks inside your fingers.
They will teach you the patience of a python.
Who can say whether oblivion is all there is?

The dying will break you or make your case.
They will draw you down a slow narrow road.
They will lift you into the light of the wind.
The day of their dying is one you can't replace.

The Minor Argonaut

I met this hospice worker
with an intoxicating laugh, sturdy hips.
Every day she knocked on my father's door.
The only language she spoke
was the language of *all in*.

With her eyes, her hands, her legs
she held fast to his body's equation:
It breaks down, the dead cells slough off
faster than the new olds grab hold.

He liked the chips she played with.

That's when I told her she was Orpheus
with the sex reversed. She smiled.
My father frowned, a little uneasy
with the fringe benefits of long distance separation.

You can say Orpheus was a minor Argonaut,
one more middling, over-ambitious artist
locked in a chamber of impotence,
a man charmed by his own despair.
But the idea of Hades never troubles him.

He arranges for his own rapid descent.
He knows his wife is not beyond reach.

She hears him. He sees her.

Whether the dark border opens or closes

is not what the story is all about.

Leaving Manzanita

Purple silhouette of Neahkahnie mountain,
our old friend with a bald spot on top.
Pacific surf, horsehair spume, unending
somersault from the beginning of the world.
Fires on the beach fed on wind and stars,
each one an encampment at land's end.
Vera, almost a woman, still a girl,
runs toward the dark, wet gleam of sand.
I want to call to her, but she vanishes
into mist or into fog or into my wanting her
to come back. *Nothing lasts, everything does.*

When Things Go Wrong on Boats

When things go wrong on boats,
they go very wrong fast.
The halyard wraps, the sheet jams,
the engine won't start,
the lee shore looms.
The waves pound at you all night.
The reef is so close you can kiss it.
Which is what you must do.
To slip past death one more time,
you must get closer to it,
so you can listen better, see sharper
the outline of your own doom.
You must do exactly the opposite
of what your parents and teachers
told you is required to survive.
When beauty and terror are equally balanced,
you must open your mouth
and kiss this force that would kill you.
Then you can move on,
shaken, humbled, grateful,
your breath no longer completely your own.

The Found Marriage

There's so much between us we can't solve.
But we know this much.
While our bodies lay down in sleep,
There comes to our bedpost,

A gathering of sparks, an exchange of signals,
An unexpected meeting, an offer of help.
You and I need so much help
To bring forth our gold.

Thankfully, the Book of Questions
Does not require a reply from the Book of Answers
And we wake with a new passion for chaos.
I kiss the points of your breasts

And trace the length of you
With the length of me.
The blind-fingered shadow
Of things unseen does not reach us

And we lay spent on bed,
Delivered from chance and carried
Through the sleepy progress
Of an afternoon nap

By the little motor of our breath,
Traveling over the earth,
Mingling with stones, stars, water.
We can't diagram this fragrance like a sentence.

We can't see the tides of night and day pulsing.
Once again we have lost our place
On the crowded page, and we're happy
To be alone again with our rain-dark breathing.

The One Wind

Mostly out of the southwest:
ten to twenty knots. The lungs of
the earth breathing me in, out,
holding me here for the night watch.
This lively wind cooks on Lake Erie.
Narragansett Bay. Penobscot Bay.
The Chesapeake. Vineyard Sound.
The Gulf of Mexico. Bahamas.
Georgian Bay. The Florida Straits.
Sir Francis Drake Channel.
Sea of Cortez. Lake Minnetonka.
I taste the wind in all those places
lying in bed, swirling it in my mouth,
my whole body seeking out its force
whipping the marsh maples and birch.
I hear through the saw of branches
and bending crowns, the one wind
kicking hard, gusting to thirty,
shivering the grasses, shining
all things to a greater exposure.
Sharpened is what it means to lie here
listening to all manner of craft
plying the channels, some approaching
harbors for the first time, others
heading out to islands they hope
will make them forget the mainland.
Exposed and sharpened, the one wind.

Stage 4

It's the catbird singing all day that you can't see,
a reminder of a noise in the body, occasionally
melodic, sealed at the outermost branches bending.
What does this stage mean? You can't go home
again? You are home? All roads are close enough.
Mostly the bars of our cage are invisible,
but they lock just the same, but not at stage four.

The Green Sleep

I left the city far behind. There was nothing more there
I could steal or lust after while the sky turned to ash.
At the folded crest between high meadow and forest
with a sliver view of the coast, I laid it all down –

the fierce quarrels with my life, the disappointments
with my body's incurable knots, the pockets of guilt,
the insistent fantasies, even the exhaustion with work
and the demands of amusement. I worried nothing,

analyzed and measured nothing, scribbled no letters
to friends nor enemies. Instead, I let the piney rise
cushion me as the salted pull of air delivered me over.
Where did I go, so purely released? Did I let death

stagger in or life live on at a greater depth of seeing?
My eyelids fluttered once. The wind over my body
circled twice, and the ancient struggle reversed its path
as the green sleep found me, in very truth, a man solved,

or rather dissolved, by not knowing what came next.

Shard

What decanter, demijohn, vial or flask
did it slip from to find me searching now?
Edges rounded, curves translucent,
this sea traveler is cut like a miniature
cobalt sail spanked from the charts.
How did it break apart to conjure up
so much of the white crest it fell from?

Imagine how far this glass
pitch-poled into the vertical sea
only to bask here, right now,
a survivor of wreckage, exiled
from its origins, sand-blasted,
wave-tumbled, so small, yet strong
enough to carry the great tonnage of a ship.

Those Who Stay,
Those Who Leave

Standing on the harbor promenade,
it's always the same longing
flashing between the red and green
channel lights: those on shore wish
they could leave for African ports.
Those leaving Cassis, cut into the calanques,
wish they could find a reason to keep
their shorelines fastened longer.
Both are lost and afraid of what
might find them tomorrow.
Where will they find the courage?
In drink, in memory, in love?
The ones who stay and the ones who leave
would have much to share should
they ever meet, but they never do,
yet they wave to one another
from the cockpit and the breakwall.
I keep no company with either hand,
but I say with certainty
we are not strangers in this brief life.

All Good Water

To be good, the water must be deep.
Deep enough to hide rocks, shoals, spits.
Wide enough to carry the swirl of ashes.
All good water. That was my father's name
for clear open stretches between islands.
Out here on the sun-bleached chart,
there's the promise of greater depth,
unexpected lifts, new freedom
from unbearable regret. Sometimes
ships are sent plunging into troughs,
never to rise again, but more often
ships break apart returning to land.
The land, the keeper of *Perpetua Secreta.*
The land, the iron in the compass.
The land, splitting open beneath you
into the old, original fires. Better
to stay out all night in the midst
of unfavorable winds. Better to slip
away quietly from the dock when no one
is watching. Better still to find
the dark glint of good water, deep water,
the water holding us for one more lovely day.

About the Author

J.P. White has published essays, articles, fiction, reviews, interviews and poetry in over a hundred publications including *The Nation, The New Republic, The Los Angeles Times Magazine, The Gettysburg Review, American Poetry Review,* and *Poetry (Chicago).* He is a graduate of New College in Sarasota, Florida, Colorado State University and Vermont College in Fine Arts. *All Good Water* is his fifth book of poems. His debut novel, *Every Boat Turns South,* was published in 2009. To learn more about J.P. White, see http://www.jpwhite.net.